MW01251034

Everyday Life

Everyday Life

Inside Ancient China

ANITA CROY

Sharpe Focus
an imprint of M.E. Sharpe, Inc.

First edition for the United States, its territories and dependencies,
Canada, Mexico, and Australia, published in 2009

Sharpe Focus
An imprint of M.E. Sharpe, Inc.
80 Business Park Drive
Armonk, NY 10504

www.sharpe-focus.com

Library of Congress Cataloging-in-Publication Data

Croy, Anita.
  Everyday life / Anita Croy.
      p. cm. -- (Inside ancient China)
  Includes bibliographical references and index.
  ISBN 978-0-7656-8170-6 (hardcover : alk. paper)
 1. China--Social life and customs--To 221 B.C.--Juvenile literature. 2.
China--Social life and customs--221 B.C.-960 A.D.--Juvenile literature. 3.
China--Social life and customs--960-1644--Juvenile literature. I. Title.

  DS741.65.C76 2009
  951'.01--dc22
                              2008031163

Editorial and design by Amber Books Ltd
Project Editor: James Bennett
Consultant Editor: Susan Whitfield
Copy Editor: Constance Novis
Picture Research: Terry Forshaw, Natascha Spargo
Design: Joe Conneally

Cover Design: Jesse M. Sanchez, M.E. Sharpe, Inc.

Printed in Malaysia

9 8 7 6 5 4 3 2 1

3 4859 00308 2608

PICTURE CREDITS
All photographs and illustrations courtesy of Shanghai Scientific and Technological Literature
Publishing House except for the following:

AKG Images: 31 (Laurent Lecat)
Alamy: 21 (dbimages), 24 (Panorama Media)
Amber Books: 22
Art Archive: 47 (Dagli Orti), 58 (Musée Guimet Paris/Dagli Orti), 61 (National Palace Museum, Taiwan),
74 (Musée Cernuschi, Paris/Dagli Orti)
Bridgeman Art Library: 8, 20 (Archives Charmet), 28 (National Museums of Scotland), 30 (Burrell
Collection, © Glasgow City Council Museums), 32 (Archives Charmet), 38/39 (Peabody Essex Museum,
Salem, Massachusetts), 40, 48, 52 (FuZhai Archive), 54 (Paul Freeman), 56/57 (The Barnes Foundation,
Merion, Pennsylvania), 60 (Victoria & Albert Museum, London)
Corbis: 12 (Redlink), 13 (Chinese Academy of Science/Reuters), 27 (Asian Art and Archaeology), 43
(Burstein Collection), 44 (Christie's Images), 67 (Christophe Boisvieux)
Dorling Kindersley: 14, 26, 36, 70, 73
Getty Images: 34 (China Span RM)
Library of Congress: 64
Photos.com: 15

All artworks courtesy of Laszlo Veres, Beehive Illustration © Amber Books
All maps courtesy of Mark Franklin © Amber Books

ABOUT THE AUTHOR
After studying modern languages, Anita Croy earned her Master's and Ph.D. degrees at University
College, University of London. Since then, she has written many books for children, specializing in
writing about Latin America and South and East Asia. Her books include *National Geographic
Investigates Ancient Pueblo* and *Solving the Mysteries of Macchu Picchu*.

Contents

Introduction

China is the world's oldest continuous civilization, originating in the plains and valleys of the Yellow and Yangtze rivers more than six thousand years ago. In the third century B.C.E., the separate kingdoms of China were united to form an empire. Over the centuries China was ruled by a series of ruling houses, or families, known as dynasties. The empire was governed by an emperor, who was advised by highly educated scholars and who commanded a strong army. No dynasty lasted for more than a few hundred years and several were founded by invaders, such as the Mongol Yuan Dynasty and the Manchu Qing Dynasty. Successive dynasties expanded Chinese territory, until the empire extended into the northern steppes, the western deserts, and the southern tropics, reaching the extent of the China we know today.

China was not always united. Often the fall of dynasties resulted in long periods where different groups competed for power. Dynasties sometimes overlapped, each controlling a part of China. Throughout all these periods, the rulers retained classical Chinese as the official language, and many dynasties saw great cultural and technological developments. Through ancient trade routes and political missions, Chinese culture reached the rest of Asia, Europe, and Africa. Chinese technologies—including the compass, paper, gunpowder, and printing—had a profound effect on civilization throughout Eurasia. China was, in turn, greatly influenced by its neighbors, resulting in a diverse and complex civilization.

Everyday Life

Ancient China was an agricultural society. Although its cities were among the largest in the world, the majority of China's population worked the land. From the earliest times, China's biggest challenge was how to feed its people and how to protect itself against raiders and conquerors on its borders. The development of irrigation systems and high-yielding crops enabled Chinese society to grow and its unique culture to develop.

Rulers tried to run the country to maximize food production and to distribute it efficiently through a network of roads, rivers, and canals. The imperial court and ruling elite were able to live in great luxury, playing chess and polo and writing poetry. But for many, life remained harsh and their only concern was to grow enough food for their families and hope that they were not caught up in war or a natural disaster.

This map shows the major cities and regions mentioned throughout this book, along with the Silk Road, linking Luoyang in the Yellow River valley with Central Asia and Europe.

The Main Dynasties of China

Shang   c. 1600–c. 1050 B.C.E.
Zhou   c. 1050–221 B.C.E.

The Zhou Dynasty can be divided into:
    Western Zhou   1050–771 B.C.E.
    Eastern Zhou   770–221 B.C.E.

    The Eastern Zhou Dynasty can also be divided into the following periods:
        Spring and Autumn Period   770–476 B.C.E.
        Warring States Period   475–221 B.C.E.

Qin   221–206 B.C.E.
Han   206 B.C.E.–220 C.E.

From 221 C.E. to 589 C.E., different regions of China were ruled by several different dynasties and emperors in a period of disunity.

Sui   589–618 C.E.
Tang   618–907 C.E.

There was another period of disunity between the Tang and Song dynasties.

Song   960–1279 C.E.
Yuan   1279–1368 C.E.
Ming   1368–1644 C.E.
Qing   1644–1911 C.E.

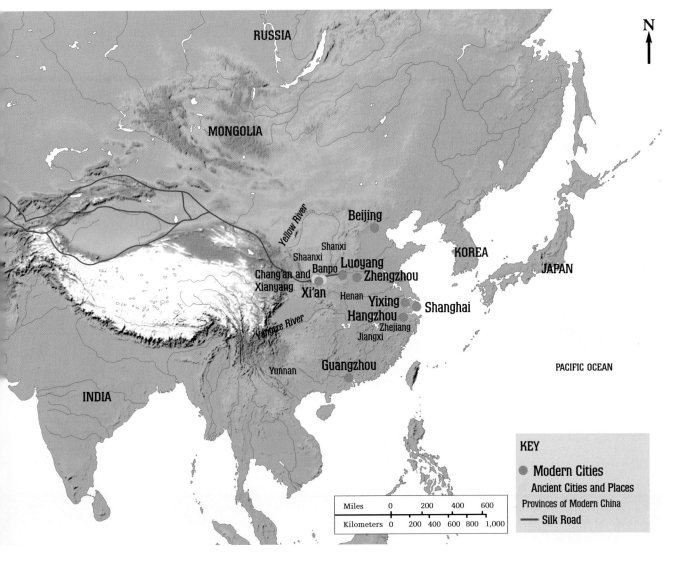

RUSSIA

N

MONGOLIA

Yellow River

Beijing

Shanxi
Shaanxi
Chang'an and
Xianyang
Banpo
Luoyang
Zhengzhou

KOREA

JAPAN

Xi'an
Henan
Yixing
Shanghai

Yangtze River
Hangzhou
Zhejiang
Jiangxi

Yunnan
Guangzhou

PACIFIC OCEAN

INDIA

Miles   0   200   400   600
Kilometers 0 200 400 600 800 1,000

KEY
● Modern Cities
  Ancient Cities and Places
Provinces of Modern China
—— Silk Road

Chapter One

Food and Drink

The earliest ancient Chinese settlements grew around the fertile land bordering the Yellow and Yangtze rivers. Many people lived in towns, but the majority of the population worked the land. The biggest challenge facing ancient China was how to feed its people, and as the population grew more settled and larger, the problem of feeding everyone grew as well.

By the time of the early Shang Dynasty (c. 1600–1050 B.C.E.), farmers in northern China were producing more food than was needed. Although most people were still poor and worked in agriculture, some of the people did not have to spend all their time and energy producing food, and had spare time to develop art and literature. Succeeding dynasties organized their societies to maximize food production, and a system was created to make sure enough food was grown and distributed. People at the top of the social ladder were able to enjoy the fruits of the masses' labor and pursue leisure activities, such as calligraphy and poetry.

Farmers and Farming

Most ancient Chinese farmers lived and worked on small parcels of land. In early times they were responsible to their landlord, but later their responsibilities were to the Chinese state. They had to pay taxes, serve in the army, and work for a certain number of days each year on large state projects, such as building roads and canals. This meant each family was left with little, if any, surplus and life was very hard. If a

This tenth-century wall painting at Dunhuang shows farmers working their fields using an ox-drawn plow.

rich landowner owned their land, they also had to give a large share of their harvest to their landlord. At times during Chinese history, life got too hard for the farmers and they rebelled, sometimes helping to bring down the ruling emperor. In order to avoid this, the emperors were careful not to demand too much from the majority that made up the farming population. Nevertheless there were many rebellions.

Farming Innovations

Chinese legend tells how in ancient times, Shen Nong (whose name means Divine Farmer) invented the plow. This invention allowed the ancient Chinese to stop relying on fishing and hunting for their food and to become a settled farming society. During the Han Dynasty (206 B.C.E.–220 C.E.), the government's iron foundries started to make iron blades for plows. This made plowing the land much easier, particularly when large plows were pulled by oxen. Around the fourth century B.C.E., a new arrangement, the trace harness (a strap fitted across the chest of the horse or ox rather than its neck), was devised and it at least doubled the load an animal was comfortably able to pull. Two hundred years later the Chinese had improved on this with the collar harness, in which a padded collar is placed around the neck of the horse or ox, allowing it to pull even heavier loads.

Different Crops

The invention of the plow probably had the single greatest influence on the appearance of the landscape of ancient China. As farmers perfected growing techniques, they carved up the landscape to grow different crops suited to their local environment.

Different crops were grown in northern and southern China. In the north, as well as some flat plains, much of the land is mountainous, with steep sides. Farmers cut terraces into the sides of the hills. The land was very fertile because it was covered in a rich yellow soil, known as loess, which blew across from the west, but there was less access to water. The farmers grew millet and wheat because these crops were better suited to the long narrow fields that they plowed around the hills and to the drier conditions. Wheat was not native to China but was brought from Central Asia as early as the third millennium B.C.E.

Hard Labor

Ancient Chinese families worked the land by hand. Every family member was involved in some aspect of farming, particularly at harvest time. They hoed the land, planted seeds, and then harvested their crops by hand. They transported water in buckets. To grind the grain they used manually operated mills. Over centuries, farming techniques modernized gradually with the introduction of beasts of burden, plows, and irrigation systems.

Irrigating the Land

The earliest irrigation machines came into use in ancient China during the Han Dynasty (206 B.C.E.–220 C.E.). They helped speed up the watering process enormously because two people working an irrigation machine could irrigate hundreds of plots of land. The most widely used was known as the "endless chain" or "turnover wheels," where two farmers stood on top of the machine and pedaled. The machine could also be powered by hand or by animals or waterwheels. The pedals turned a large cogwheel, which, in turn, pulled a chain of square wooden pallets. The chain pulled the full wooden pallets uphill from a canal. At their highest point the pallets emptied their load of water into a wooden channel. The water then flowed out of the front end of the machine into an irrigation ditch at a higher level.

The system was used successfully in both northern and southern China. In mountainous areas, where crops were farmed on terraces instead of in fields, water was brought to the steep terraces from wells and canals using the irrigation machines.

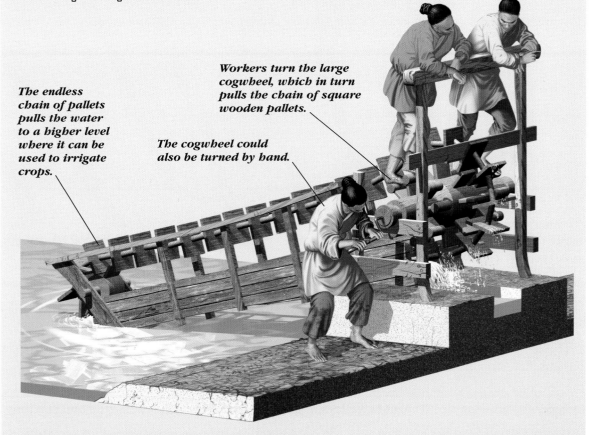

Workers turn the large cogwheel, which in turn pulls the chain of square wooden pallets.

The endless chain of pallets pulls the water to a higher level where it can be used to irrigate crops.

The cogwheel could also be turned by hand.

The introduction of irrigation machines made life much easier for the ancient Chinese farmer. This square-pallet chain pump, also known as the "endless chain" or the "turnover wheels," was the most popular kind of irrigation machine.

These rice-growing terraces in Longji are carved straight into the hillside, a practice that dates back more than 650 years.

The south was a land of mountains and lakes. Plenty of water was available, providing ideal growing conditions for rice and even for raising fish. The irrigation systems used by the farmers here created a vast patchwork of flooded fields, known as paddy fields. However, as they became more sophisticated in their crop cultivation, the southern Chinese also sculpted terraces for growing rice. The many valleys of the Yangtze River were very fertile and starting from the time of the Tang Dynasty (618–907 c.e.) provided most of the empire's food. During the Song Dynasty (960–1279 c.e.) the Chinese learned about even faster ways of growing rice from their neighbors in the country of Cham (present-day Vietnam and Cambodia) and so were able to increase their rice production further still. People in northern China started to eat more rice after this time, too.

Chinese Cooking

The art of Chinese cooking dates back more than two thousand years. Growing, preparing, and cooking food took up much of the day for most families. A person's diet depended on their income, but no matter which social class they belonged to, it was usual to eat two meals a day. One meal was eaten in the middle of the morning, and the other before dark.

Rich Chinese people enjoyed lavish banquets while ordinary people survived on a diet of beans, grains, and vegetables. For them, meat was a luxury. Rice was a staple in the south, whereas in northern China people ate more millet and wheat. However, as transportation links improved, rice grown in the south was taken north for consumption. Fish was plentiful and widely eaten. New foods came in from Central Asia, such as grapes, sesame, and alfalfa. Both rich and poor Chinese people used a range of different herbs and spices to flavor their food. Ginger, for example, which grows in China, was originally used in cooking to disguise the smell of bad meat. Food was cut into small pieces and cooked rapidly (stir-fried) in a *wok*, a

Noodles have been a popular food in China for thousands of years. These dried noodles are around 4,000 years old and were found, preserved, in an overturned sealed bowl close to the Yellow River.

type of deep, rounded iron skillet, because it cooked quicker and used less fuel than other means of cooking.

The ancient Chinese often left food out in the sun to dry out so that it could be eaten at a later date. When they wanted to cook the dried food, they first soaked it in cold water. One of the staple foods of ancient China was the noodle. These were made from wheat, bean, or rice flour mixed with water and then allowed to dry.

Starting as early as the sixth century B.C.E., writers and philosophers took a great interest in cooking. For example, Confucius (551–479 B.C.E.) advised that rulers should govern as one would cook a fish, that is,

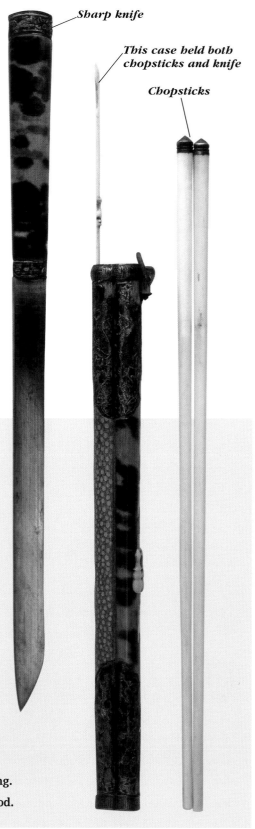

Sharp knife

This case held both chopsticks and knife

Chopsticks

Chopsticks

In ancient times people ate with their hands, tearing meat from bones with knives or their teeth and scooping up rice and grain with their fingers. Later, Chinese food was sliced and chopped into small pieces so that people did not need knives to cut up their food at the table. Instead, they used chopsticks.

The earliest chopsticks, which were made from two pieces of very thin wood or bamboo, became widely used during the Han Dynasty (206 B.C.E.–220 C.E.) but were probably developed much earlier. By 500 C.E., the use of chopsticks had spread from China to the neighboring countries of Japan, Korea, and Vietnam.

A sharp knife was one of the main tools of Chinese cooking. Chopsticks could be used in both preparing and eating food.

Spices

By combining different herbs and spices, Chinese cooks were able to create sweet, sour, bitter, spicy, and salty flavors. Typical flavorings included chili peppers—originally introduced from south America—which were added to dishes in southwestern China to make them hot and spicy. Star anise, recognizable by its star shape, was a popular flavoring, as were sesame seeds—originally from central Asia—which were sprinkled on both sweet and savory foods. To flavor sweet foods, flower petals and tangerine peel were used.

Star anise, a popular flavoring in Chinese cooking, is harvested from the *Illicium verum* shrub which is native to China.

with little fuss and as delicately as possible. In writings such as the *Shijing* (Classic of Poetry), poems describe banquets and their drunken guests.

Mention of food and wine was not restricted to poets and philosophers. Jia Sixie (*Jee'ah-suh-shee'eh*), for example, was the author of China's first agricultural encyclopedia, *Essential Skills for the Common People*, which has been dated to about 540 C.E. In his book he included 280 recipes, apparently gathered from earlier recipe books. He followed the time-honored method of listing ingredients, quantities, preparation time, and how to prepare and serve the various dishes. His recipes included how to make cottage cheese as well as how to cook roast meat, stews, noodles, and breads. An even earlier cookbook was discovered as recently as 1999. During excavations of the tomb of Wu Yang (who died in 162 B.C.E.), in present-day Hunan province, archaeologists discovered around 300 bamboo strips with at least 155 different

This image, painted directly onto a brick, shows a person cooking. The brick was part of a tomb dating back to the period of disunity following the Han Dynasty.

recipes written on them. Of these, 148 were for different meat recipes, including one for suckling pig. The text tells how to kill the pig, remove its hair, and clean it, and then explains the different stages of steaming and boiling the meat before cooking it with a sweet beef broth made from wine, salt, meat stock, ginger, and magnolia bark. According to the bamboo texts, the same recipe could be used to cook horse, lamb, or venison.

The period of seven centuries between these two cookbooks saw many of the major changes that were to take place in Chinese cooking. Probably the biggest change was the introduction of rice in the fourth century and its subsequent availability in northern China once the

The Silk Road

Throughout the first millennium C.E., trade between China and India and the West thrived along trade routes running across Eurasia, which were later referred to collectively as the Silk Road. Very few people ever traveled the entire Silk Road. Instead, traders traveled along one section only, and sold goods to be carried to the next trading point by another merchant. Merchants rode in huge caravans of carts and camels laden with goods, and faced great dangers such as crossing war zones, being attacked by bandits, and encountering deadly desert storms. However, they could stop to buy supplies and rest their animals at desert oasis towns or at roadside inns called caravanserai. Communities of foreign merchants, such as the Sogdians, who came from a kingdom west of China, took up residence in Chinese cities like the Tang capital, Chang'an. All kinds of goods were traded, including silk and textiles, precious stones and jewels, foods, animals, plants, perfumes, and medicines.

country was unified and improved transportation systems allowed it to be brought from the south. The other major change took place during the Tang Dynasty (618–907 C.E.) with the introduction of another crop, tea, which was produced in the south, and the introduction of many foods from Central Asia and from other lands along the Silk Road, including wine made from grapes.

Feasts and Banquets

While most of the ancient Chinese population ate the same daily diet of grain and vegetables, with meat on occasion, rich Chinese people ate and drank the finest foods money could buy. Banquets were held to celebrate many different events. The Chinese New Year and the Moon Festival were two of the important annual dates that merited a banquet. Weddings were celebrated with a banquet, while the dead were also honored with feasts during the year.

The lavishness of a banquet or feast depended on the occasion. Imperial banquets were the most opulent, and only the finest foods and drink were served. Ceremonial banquets varied from extravagant to simple, while the banquets of noble families could be very grand affairs. The differing banquets shared some common traits. Food was served to the guests by servants and meals lasted many hours. Rice was not the main feature of the meal but was served last. It was often not eaten at all, because the guests had filled up on the meats and fish served earlier in the meal. Vegetables were eaten as side dishes, as were different grains. Unlike meals eaten every day, food at banquets was served one course after another—not brought to the table all at once—and might consist of more than twenty different dishes.

Banquet Etiquette

In ancient China, there were strict rules about behavior at banquets. For example, guests were expected to be very respectful to their host. During the Song Dynasty (960–1279 C.E.), Emperor Zhengzong (968–1022 C.E.) issued an order that set out the rules of acceptable behavior, or etiquette, at imperial banquets. He ordered that diners dress and behave appropriately. They had to sit according to their social position, and could only speak at certain points. In order to enforce these rules, there were etiquette

This ancient Chinese painting shows three men enjoying a sumptuous feast consisting of many different dishes.

inspectors whose job was to enforce correct behavior. The problem for diners was remembering all the many different rules. In fact, there were more rules for how to behave at a banquet than there were for how to conduct warfare.

The importance attached to etiquette came, as with many things, from Confucius (551–479 B.C.E.), who decreed that etiquette and laws should rule people. Another philosopher, Xunzi (313–238 B.C.E.), said, "A man without etiquette cannot survive; a business without etiquette cannot succeed; and a country without etiquette can have no peace."

Drinking Tea

Written references to tea in Chinese literature date back five thousand years, though the exact moment when people started to drink tea remains unclear. It is known that the earliest records of tea harvesting date from around 2000 B.C.E. By then, drinking tea was already an established custom. According to ancient Chinese legend, drinking tea dates back to 2737 B.C.E., when a blossom from a camellia tree fell into a cup of boiled drinking water belonging to Shen Nong (the Divine Farmer). He was feeling tired but after he had drunk his water with the camellia flower he felt alert and awake, which made him wonder about the special properties of the leaf.

By the time of the Han Dynasty (206 B.C.E.–220 C.E.), people were already drinking tea for medicinal purposes and at the royal court, but it tasted very bitter. Before then, warm rice beer was the most popular drink. However, improvements in the way tea was collected and brewed helped improve its flavor—and popularity. Tea became the drink of choice at the royal courts by the time of the Three Kingdoms (221–277 C.E.). There is a story that tells how tea came to replace rice wine as the drink of the royal courts. A king offered wine to his guests at a banquet but one guest refused the wine because it made him drunk. He was given tea instead, and from then on, the king always served tea at his banquets for those who preferred it. He also offered tea as gifts, which helped spread the reputation of tea.

The Etiquette of Eating

The etiquette of eating covered every aspect of a banquet, from sending out invitations to the positioning of food for guests to eat. Everything was arranged according to which guests were the most senior and honorable, who would be seated in the best position at the table, served first, and given the first choice of the food. Rules extended to whether guests could burp, slurp, or pick their teeth during a meal. Even the presentation of dishes was governed by etiquette. For example, it was considered good manners to serve a fish with the tail facing the honored guest. Many of these practices still apply at banquets in China today.

It was during the Tang Dynasty (618–907 C.E.) that tea became the national drink. Initially, tea drinking was limited to the areas where the tea bush grew, in southern China. At that time, it was drunk after a meal because it was seen as possessing medicinal properties that aided digestion.

Tea drinking became popular among Buddhist monks because it helped them stay awake during meditation. During the eighth century, a poet and Buddhist priest named Lu Yu (733–804 C.E.) wrote a book entitled *The Classic Art of Tea*. In it, he described the proper way of brewing, steeping, and serving the tea leaves. He maintained that tea should be brewed with water from a slow-moving stream in a pottery cup. He even specified the best location for drinking tea, which was in a pavilion overlooking a lily pond. Following the publication of the book, tea drinking took on a greater significance. Poets and writers wrote about tea and emperors gave tea as gifts. Buildings specially for tea drinking were built and soon teahouses became a common sight across China.

Cha

The Chinese name for tea is *cha*, which is the same word as the Chinese character that means to test, investigate, or check. Later, a new character, also pronounced *cha*, was created. It had wood at the bottom, and flowers and grass at the top with a man in between the two. This was meant to show how tea could bring man and nature into balance.

The symbol for *cha* clearly shows the different parts that made up the character.

The golden age of tea drinking occurred during the Song Dynasty (960–1279 C.E.). Emperor Huizong (1082–1135 C.E.), who reigned 1101–1125 C.E., wrote *Daguanchalun* (Treatise on Tea). In this essay he wrote about how to grow, process, brew, and drink tea. He told his people to enjoy the benefits of drinking tea, which brought peace and quiet to the mind.

A tea-drinking culture emerged with people from different regions across China developing their own ways of brewing, serving, and drinking tea. Initially, leaves from the tea bush were pounded into a ball or brick shape and then added to water. During the Song Dynasty, people started to use loose tea leaves. Tea specialists discovered that the kind of pot the tea was brewed in and the cup it was drunk from also affected the taste of the tea. Potters made teacups or bowls designed specifically for drinking tea, which were highly prized.

This Qing Dynasty (1644–1911 C.E.) painting on silk shows a family in their garden welcoming visitors with tea served from an elegant teapot and porcelain cups.

During the Ming Dynasty (1368–1644 C.E.), different methods of drying the loose leaves were investigated. The ancient Chinese were starting to export tea to the rest of the world at this time and it had to be dried before being transported on the long sea journeys. Also during the Ming Dynasty, people became interested in finding the perfect ceramic teapot and drinking cup. Craftsmen experimented with different ways of firing the clay to make fine, heat-resistant ceramics. Tea tasting also became a recognized profession and tea competitions were popular.

Gongfu Tea-Brewing Method

This method of brewing became popular in China during the Ming Dynasty (1368–1644 C.E.). It was also during this time that craftsmen from Yixing (*ee-shing*) began producing porous clay teapots, which helped improve the flavor of the tea. The fundamental difference between *Gongfu* brewing and "regular" brewing is in the amount of tea used and the length of time it is left to steep. The *Gongfu* method used more tea, but it was left to infuse for a very short time. For regular tea brewing a smaller quantity was used but it was left to brew for longer.

Large amounts of land in China are still given over to tea cultivation, as it remains the most popular drink. Different types of tea are grown at different elevations and in different regions.

Chapter Two

Clothes and Jewelry

The way the ancient Chinese dressed varied dramatically according to their social position and income. Ancient Chinese society was arranged in a formal social order with the emperor at the top and the peasants at the bottom. It was considered very important that different ranks and social classes were immediately apparent to everyone, and the easiest way of telling a person's social rank was by how they dressed.

Clothes, jewelry, and even hair styles were used to show what position a person held in society. However, for the majority of Chinese people, especially those who worked on the land, clothing changed little over the centuries. Peasants initially wore practical clothes made from hemp, a fabric woven from plant fiber that was cheap to produce, until cotton eventually replaced it during the Song (960–1279 C.E.) and Yuan (1279–1368 C.E.) dynasties.

The clothes of the rich and the nobility were made of silk. The Chinese discovered silk and exported it to the rest of the world along the land and sea trade routes known as the Silk Road. During periods of peace and increasing prosperity, for example, during the Tang Dynasty (618–907 C.E.), clothing became more luxurious. However, there were few changes in the basic shape of clothing over the centuries.

These illustrations show members of the ruling elite, an official, and servants during the Qing Dynasty (1644–1911 C.E.). The clothing of the seated aristocrats is much more highly decorated than the relatively plain clothes of the official and servants.

These finely embroidered women's shoes were discovered in a grave along the Silk Road in western China.

Shoes were very important to the ancient Chinese. Everyone wore shoes including peasants, who wore straw sandals. The nobility wore shoes made from cloth or leather—or even silk for wearing around the home. They were often embroidered and had silk linings for comfort.

Lifestyle Influences Clothing

People in different parts of China had different ways of life, and this had an influence on the styles of clothing they wore. While most of the basic items of clothing, worn on a daily basis, developed on the plains of northern China, silk from central and southern China transformed clothing for the rich. The horse-riding nomads of northern and western China, for example, introduced functional clothes like pants. And everyone, no matter how poor they were, wore a hat and shoes.

Jewelry was another means of showing a person's social status, although the lavishness and detail of embroidery on clothing was often a more immediate way of telling a person's rank.

How Do We Know What People Wore in Ancient China?

Our knowledge of clothing in ancient China comes from different sources. Tombs are valuable resources for information about clothing worn in ancient times because they contain clothing that has been protected in dry conditions. The clothes of those buried with their masters give an indication of what ordinary people wore, and the many ceramic figurines found in tombs showed how fashions changed. Paintings on the walls of tombs and in Buddhist paintings also gave an insight into what people wore in ancient China.

These two officials of the Ming Dynasty (1368–1644 C.E.) are wearing brightly colored robes. Officials were allowed to wear robes of purple, red, green, or blue, while yellow was reserved for the emperor. Ordinary people were only allowed to wear muted blue or black clothing.

Officials wore a headscarf with ear flaps called a futou. *Supposedly, if officials started to whisper in court, the flaps would knock together, alerting the emperor. This was meant to prevent officials from making power alliances with each other.*

Both of these high-ranking officials are wearing clothes embroidered with elaborate animal designs. The animal depicted the rank of the official.

This book illustration shows a Qing Dynasty official alongside two women being transported in a kind of passenger wheelbarrow by a servant. The rank of each person is clear from their different clothes.

The ancient Chinese had certain ideas about the very special nature of hair. They never cut it because the great Chinese philosopher Confucius (551–479 B.C.E.) said, "One should never damage the body, including the skin and hair, because all are bestowed by one's parents. This is the fundamental principle of filial piety." This Confucian teaching, of treasuring one's hair as much as one's life, continued until modern times.

Hemp

Hemp is one of the oldest of all Chinese crops, and archeological discoveries have proved that hemp was used for a very long time. Fragments of pottery found at the site of the ancient village of Banpo near present-day Xi'an have imprints of hemp textiles on them, which date from 5,000 years ago. Hemp fabric has also been uncovered in different tombs. A piece of hemp textile, decorated with a silver-white design, was found in a cliff tomb near Guixi (*Gweh-shee*) in Jiangxi province. It was produced sometime between 770–221 B.C.E. As well as making clothes, hats, and shoes from hemp, the Chinese made paper from it, ate it, and used it as a medicine. Hemp cloth was used at every stage of life, from wrapping a newborn baby to funeral shrouds for a dead body.

Clothing of Poor People

The basic item of clothing was a tunic, similar to a long t-shirt. Women wore long tunics that reached to the ground and men wore shorter, knee-length tunics, fastened with a belt. During the cold winters, people wore padded jackets over the tunics and pants underneath. Clothes had to be practical. Most Chinese worked in the fields and the clothes had to keep them warm and not interfere with hoeing, sowing seeds, and irrigating the land.

The clothes were made from hemp or ramie. Ramie belongs to the nettle family and is also known as Chinese grass. Along with silk, ramie and hemp were the main textiles until the Song (960–1279 C.E.) and Yuan (1279–1368 C.E.) dynasties, when cotton became more popular. The ancient Chinese were reluctant to grow cotton, which had arrived from India by 200 B.C.E. and was grown along the Silk Road, but the Mongol invasions of the thirteenth century destroyed many of the mulberry trees needed to produce the valuable silk. To make up for the reduction in silk production, Mongol rulers, like Kublai Khan (1215–1294 C.E.), ordered the growing of cotton plants to replace silk production. In 1289 C.E., the Mongol rulers opened training centers to teach farmers how to grow cotton. To encourage them, a law was passed in 1296 C.E. that allowed farmers who grew cotton to pay lower taxes. Before long, cotton became more popular than ramie or hemp, and soon became the fabric used for the clothing of the majority of the population.

Poor people's clothing was dull in color. During the sixth century an emperor of the Sui Dynasty (589–618 C.E.) decreed that poor people could only wear clothing that was muted blue or black, and rich people could wear brighter colors, principally red and blue.

This bronze lamp figurine of a kneeling servant girl was found in a tomb dating from the Han Dynasty (206 B.C.E.–220 C.E.). She is wearing the typical Hanfu-style of dress of the day.

Silk

The exact date of the discovery of silk is not known. We do know, however, that silk was made exclusively in China for thousands of years before other countries started to produce it. Historians believe silk production dates back to 4000 B.C.E. Stones have been discovered that were etched during the Han Dynasty (206 B.C.E.–220 C.E.), showing the production of silk. By the time of the Han Dynasty silk production was very sophisticated and the items produced were of the highest quality.

The famous Silk Road, as it came to be known, began in the second century B.C.E. Jade, tea, spices, and countless other items were transported along this route to be traded abroad. Silk was exported to Rome as early as the first century C.E., when it was literally worth its weight in gold.

According to Chinese legend, one of the wives of the mythological Huang Di (whose name means Yellow Emperor) discovered silk 4,700 years ago. There are different stories about how she stumbled across the making of silk. One version tells that a cocoon dropped into her cup of tea while she was sitting in the garden. Another version has it that she was trying to work out why the emperor's mulberry trees had been damaged. She discovered silkworms were eating the leaves and building cocoons. She put a cocoon into hot water and was surprised to see a single thread unwind. The thread was long, strong, and flexible and she was soon weaving silk threads to make clothing.

In fact, silkworms eat huge quantities of mulberry leaves (one ton of leaves are needed to produce around six pounds or 2.7 kilograms of silk). To produce enough silk, the ancient Chinese planted mulberry tree orchards and crossbred them so the trees would grow lots of leaves for the worms to eat, but not many berries. They also learned that the timing of removing the thread from the cocoon is crucial.

This silk robe dates from the late nineteenth century. We can tell that it was worn by a member of the Imperial Court because of the imperial dragons and twelve symbols of Imperial Authority embroidered on it.

The Clothing of the Wealthy

Rich people in ancient China wore brightly colored, elaborately decorated, luxurious silk clothing. During the Shang Dynasty (c. 1600–1050 B.C.E.) a long silk robe became the basic piece of clothing for both the men and women of the nobility, and was worn up until modern times. Silk was used because it was luxurious and beautiful, but it also kept the wearer cool in the summer and warm in the winter. It could be dyed in any color using plant dyes, but bright yellow was reserved for the exclusive use of the emperor.

During the Western Zhou Dynasty (c. 1050–771 B.C.E.), the more senior a person's position the more ornately he dressed. Details that could be changed included the length of the skirt, the width of a sleeve, and the amount of embroidery on the fabric, all of which were used to show a person's social position. Buttons were not used at the time so jewelry, such as a jade ornament, was used to keep the coat closed. Later, during the Eastern Zhou Dynasty (770–221 B.C.E.), a new style of robe was designed, known as a *shenyi*. Everyone, no matter what social position, gender, or profession, wore the *shenyi*. However, the elite still stood out by wearing more sumptuous, highly decorated fabrics.

Hairstyles and Decorations

The way the ancient Chinese wore their hair was an important part of their daily dress. The poor did not have the chance to do anything to decorate their hair, but for the rich there were many ways of making their hair as attractive as possible. Men as well as women wore their hair long. Men tied their hair and wore it in a topknot, while women had much more elaborate hairstyles held in place by combs and hairpins. Rich women decorated their hair with beautiful hairpins made from gold, silver, jade, and glass, and it was not unusual for women in the emperor's court to spend a number of hours each morning having their hair arranged. Girls usually wore their hair in two coils or braids, while small boys wore their hair in braids.

Beauty

The idea of what was considered to be female beauty changed with different dynasties. Generally speaking, women were expected to have red lips, fair skin, and thin black eyebrows. To achieve this, they added color to

A Fatal Cut?

At the end of the Han Dynasty (206 B.C.E.–220 C.E.) a warlord named Cao Cao (155–220 C.E.) issued a command to his armies that forbade them to tread on any crops, the penalty being decapitation (chopping off the head). Soon after, the warlord's horse bolted, and galloped over farmland, spoiling fields full of seeds. Cao Cao insisted he must receive his punishment just like anyone else, but his soldiers did not dare execute him. Cao Cao eventually thought of a compromise. Instead of having his head cut off, he cut off his hair, which in ancient China was a severe penalty.

This painting on silk from the early Qing Dynasty shows a lady having her hair prepared by her maid.

their lips and powder to their faces. They often shaved off their eyebrows, or plucked them finely with tweezers and then painted them in using kohl pigment. The painted eyebrows were called "moth eyebrows" and often praised by poets as a sign of beauty. A woman's hair was expected to be black and shiny, her waist small, and her feet tiny.

Among the wealthy, it was considered fashionable to keep the fingernails long, and it was a common practice for both wealthy men and women to grow the nails of their little fingers to a great length. To protect the nail, they wore ornate, highly decorated nail guards made from silver and even gold. A long nail was seen as a sign of wealth because a person with such a long nail could not do any manual work. During the thirteenth century, women stained their fingernails with a mixture made from pink balsam leaves crushed in alum. This was an early kind of nail polish that had to be reapplied at least every six weeks.

Jiaoling youren: crossed collar. The shenyi was always folded onto the right side. The left was only for corpses. —

Qu: sleeve cuffs.

The Shenyi

The *shenyi* was made up of two principal parts, a tunic and skirt. During the Shang Dynasty (c. 1600–1050 B.C.E.), basic clothing consisted of a tunic to the knee worn over an ankle-length skirt. The cuffs of the coat sleeves were narrow and the tunic had no buttons. Instead, it was kept closed by a wide sash or belt. Hanging from the waist sash was another piece of fabric, called the *bixi (Bee-she)*, which reached to the knees. It was notable for its brightly colored fabric, made from the primary colors of red, blue, or green silk. The shape of the *shenyi* remained largely unaltered throughout history, though small details changed.

Much of what we know about ancient Chinese dress comes from wood and terracotta figures found in tombs. Many were painted, which gives us an idea of the colors and decoration of ancient Chinese textiles.

This colored engraving shows a woman binding her own feet, a practice which only died out in the twentieth century.

Foot Binding

The ancient Chinese custom of binding girls' feet started in the Song Dynasty (960–1279 C.E.) and did not become widespread immediately, but it did continue to modern times. The ancient Chinese believed that tiny feet were an important part of a woman's beauty, so the feet of the wealthy women were bound from the age of around four or five, with their big toes being bent and bound under the foot. The practice left the women unable to walk properly, so anyone who needed to work for a living did not have their feet bound.

Jewelry

The earliest inhabitants of present-day China wore jewelry. We know this because archaeologists have unearthed shells with holes drilled into them, along with stone beads. Both men and women in ancient China wore jewelry. From early on, men wore belt hooks and plaques while women wore ornate hairpins and combs along with headdresses. The long sleeves and high necks of the *shenyi* left little room for the wearer to display jewelry, and as a result necklaces, rings, and earrings were worn less often. In later times, jewelry was an important part of court officials' clothing and strict laws regulated exactly what they could wear. These rules did not apply to women, and their jewelry became more beautiful and flamboyant as gold, precious stones, and pearls were used.

Belts were held in place with hooks. This dragon hook was made from jade and discovered in a Han Dynasty tomb in Guangzhou.

Belts and belt hooks were probably introduced to China around the fourth century B.C.E. from one of the neighboring tribes such as the Xiongnu (*Shee'ong-noo*) nomads. Men's belt hooks could be very ornate. Originally, the earliest hooks were made from bronze and often inlaid with precious metals, such as gold and silver. They were made in all kinds of different shapes, including musical instruments and insects. Belts were decorated with highly adorned buckles also made from precious metals. Weights were sewn into the long sleeves of silk robes to prevent them from flapping around and to help them hang properly. Even though they could not be seen, these too were made of bronze and in different designs, such as birds.

Gold was the most highly valued material for jewelry after jade, and was used in bracelets and necklaces. These were often inset with jade and other precious stones. Often, jewelry was engraved with lucky symbols. These symbols were supposed to bring good luck to the wearer and to keep away evil spirits.

Chapter Three

At Home

From the earliest times, ancient Chinese homes were built to keep their owners warm, but their design varied enormously depending on their location and how much money the family had. We know from paintings and artifacts found in tombs of the Shang Dynasty (c.1600–1050 B.C.E.), that the royal families of the early Chinese dynasties, noblemen, and officials lived in great splendor. Furniture, carpets, and different domestic objects hint at the extravagance and luxury of Chinese royal courts and noble houses. However, it is much harder to find information about how the majority of Chinese people, like the farmers and workers, lived because their houses have long since disappeared and they had few possessions.

Because China is such a big country with different climates, from the cold mountains in the north to the steamy tropics in the south, the housing people needed varied from province to province. In Shaanxi (*Shaarn-shee*) province in central China where temperatures often fell below freezing, farmers built homes in caves on the side of a mountain to try and keep warm. In southern China, some villagers built their homes on stilts so that when the river flooded their homes did not. In northern China, homes were built with thick walls to keep in the warmth and large courtyards to allow as much sunlight as possible to enter the home. In the south, where it was necessary to keep out as much of the sun as possible and create maximum ventilation, houses were built with smaller windows and large overhanging roofs.

The main entrance to a courtyard house in Shanxi province. The walls and double doors conceal the home from public gaze.

In ancient China it was normal, in both rich and poor families, for more than one generation to live together. In the poorest homes, all the family lived in one room. In houses of more than one room, no matter what the family income or position, the organization of the house was arranged along a strict hierarchy. The oldest, and therefore most respected, member of the family, usually the head of the household, lived in the main building with other family members living in additional buildings. Ancient Chinese homes were built in such a way that they could easily be added to as the family grew or became wealthier. Houses were always oriented to the south to avoid the cold winds coming from the north.

Houses were built, if possible, on platforms of stamped earth, brick, or stone to keep the floor level away from the damp earth. The courtyard house, divided into different sections by courtyards, was a typical kind of Chinese home. The biggest houses had many courtyards and houses for the extended family. The main family lived at the center of the complex and the inner courtyard was reserved for them. The outer rooms were for other family members, while rich families needed space for their many servants. Some homes had a garden, and a wall surrounded most of them to serve as both protection and to mark out boundaries.

Neolithic settlements in the Yellow River valley would have consisted of simple dwellings like this, made from bamboo. A central hole in the roof allowed smoke from the fire to escape.

Towns were built on a grid system and areas were divided into wards. Walls with gates, which were locked each night, surrounded each ward. Every evening, a drum would be struck to warn the residents that the gates were closing. If their visitors did not leave in time they would be locked in and have to spend the night.

Homes of the Poor

Most people in ancient China were poor and lived in the countryside. Their homes were temporary structures that eventually fell apart and disintegrated if they were not knocked down and replaced by a new building. A typical peasant home was built from bamboo and stamped dirt, which means that none have survived. Roofs were made from straw, and the only light came from the door and window, if there was one. There was a fire pit for cooking and warmth in the middle of the sunken floor. We know a lot about houses from Neolithic times (10,000–2000 B.C.E.) because of the excavations at Banpo in Yangshao province. These reveal that houses were built with sunken floors to keep in heat. From the ninth century B.C.E., roofs were thatched and covered buildings that could be several stories high. The roofs sloped

The Dai people of Yunnan province in southwest China live in bamboo stilt houses. This style of house dates back 1,000 years. The family lives on the upper level and keeps livestock on the ground level.

This eighteenth-century painting shows the affluence of the city of Guangzhou, with its many courtyard houses packed closely along the Pearl River. Guangzhou has been an important trading port since ancient times.

so that rainwater could run off, and were held up by a system of brackets that became more complicated over the centuries.

Peasants often had two homes, not because they were rich but because during the summer they lived in a temporary structure close to their land so they could harvest. During the winter, they moved to their permanent home, which was a more substantial structure.

During the thirteenth century many people in large cities, such as Hangzhou, in Zhejiang (*Juh-jee'ang*) province, lived in buildings of eight to ten stories. Hangzhou then had a population of two million people, forty times more than the largest European city at the time. They paid rent to their landlord or to the state. These structures were built straight onto narrow cobblestone

streets. On the first floor was a store or a craftsman's workshop. The family lived above. There were no bathrooms; instead the family used a bucket, which was collected each morning and used to fertilize neighboring fields. Many of the poorest members of society lived with as many as seven people in one room, while beggars lived on the streets.

The houses of the poor changed little over subsequent dynasties, while the homes of the rich and nobility changed during the Qin (*Chin*) Dynasty (221–206 B.C.E.), and then changed little after that. The ordinary people tended to live on the edges of towns and villages. The center of the town was reserved for the large houses of the ruling families, landowners, and rich merchants. Over centuries, the gap between the very rich and the poor in ancient China grew. The poor families continued to live in small huts with sunken floors and thatched roofs as the rich built ever more magnificent mansions. While the rich furnished their homes with beautiful pieces of furniture, carpets, and paintings, the homes of poor families contained almost nothing.

A Nobleman's Home in the Han Dynasty (206 B.C.E.–220 C.E.)

Over the centuries, the homes of noblemen became more lavish. Building materials improved and homes became another way of displaying wealth. During the Han Dynasty, a popular type of dwelling was the two-story courtyard house, which had its own watchtower. These houses were built with intersecting crossbeams and rafters. They were highly decorated and carved on all the visible surfaces. The floors were covered with woolen rugs and embroidered cushions, which were much more luxurious than the animal skins and mats made of grass that their ancestors had put on the floors.

The family slept on beds built from the best quality timber, draped with embroidered cloths. Hand-carved screens were used to give the family more privacy. A wall surrounded the house, which also housed the family's servants. Courtyards divided up the space and gave the family some room outdoors to grow plants and keep animals. The complex could also contain offices for the family and the watchtower. Watchtowers were common because the authorities used them to keep a close eye on the local residents.

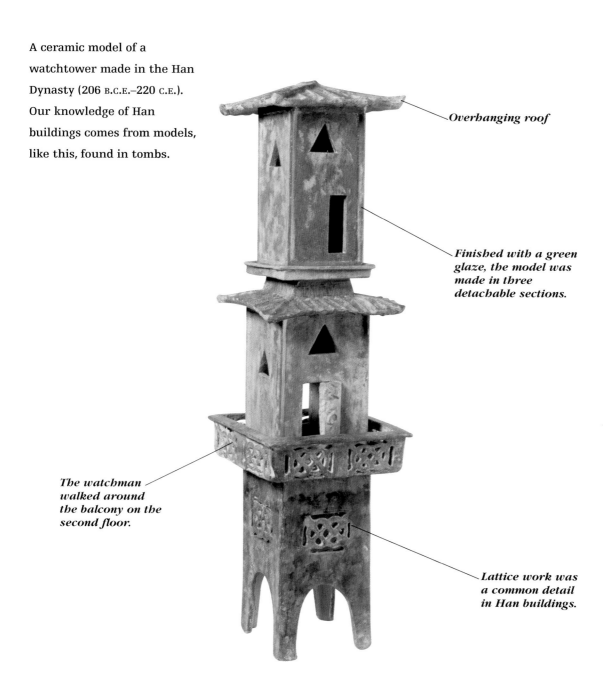

A ceramic model of a watchtower made in the Han Dynasty (206 B.C.E.–220 C.E.). Our knowledge of Han buildings comes from models, like this, found in tombs.

Overhanging roof

Finished with a green glaze, the model was made in three detachable sections.

The watchman walked around the balcony on the second floor.

Lattice work was a common detail in Han buildings.

A Nobleman's House in the Song Dynasty (960–1279 c.e.)

By the time of the Song Dynasty, there was a very big difference between the houses of the rich and the poor. For the noblemen and wealthy, houses were made up of a collection of buildings. The different buildings were either set at right angles or built one behind the other. Between the buildings were courtyards. The buildings were usually raised above the courtyards to keep the houses dry when it rained. The main entrance was through a gate, and there were strict rules about the size and design of a gate. For example, only the emperor could have a gate with several entrances. In front of the gate was a screen, which was meant to keep out the bad spirits who were thought to be able to walk in straight lines only and not turn corners. On either side of the gate were posts decorated with images of the gate gods who protected the house.

Within the courtyard complex, in addition to the residential buildings, a nobleman might build pavilions to be used for different functions. One pavilion might be to watch the moonlight, another to play music in, and another to keep the family cool during the hot weather. Gardens

A typical courtyard house with its private inner courtyard. This was once the home of the famous Chinese opera singer Mei Lanfang.

How Houses Were Built

Homes for the rich during the Song Dynasty (960–1279 C.E.) were, like those of the poor, still made without foundations or load-bearing walls. Instead, the wooden pillars, spaced about three feet (one meter) apart, were used to hold up the roof. This technique meant that the houses could be moved if needed.

All buildings were rectangular in shape. New buildings were added to existing buildings at right angles. Roofs sloped on either side and were turned up at the edges to let the rain run off. Curved roofs, by imperial order, could only be used on the houses of people of high rank and for government buildings.

were popular and extravagant. They often contained a water feature, such as an artificial pool complete with a wooden bridge. Very rich owners spent huge fortunes on using the best materials, such as imported rare woods, along with special tiles and glazed bricks to decorate their home. One wealthy resident was said to have had a floor inlaid with silver.

The interior was elegantly furnished with low tables and armchairs. Beds were lavish and walls were decorated with scrolls; antique vases were placed on display. Fresh flower arrangements in the house were an important part of home interiors in the Song Dynasty.

Furnishing the Home

The biggest change in household furnishings that took place in ancient China was the arrival of the chair. For centuries, the wealthier people of ancient China had sat on the floor on woven mats. The chair arrived in China with Buddhism in the first or second century C.E. but was not in common use until the tenth century. Few, if any, early forms of furniture survive, but we have some idea of what they looked like because of paintings on tomb walls and furnishings found in tombs. For example, the remains of lacquer furniture dating from about 500 B.C.E. have been found in tombs.

The houses of the rich and poor were furnished very differently. The poor had little, if any, furniture at all. They slept on rush mats and used pillows made from pottery or wood to rest their heads on. They sat on the floor to eat. Because they had few possessions, they did not need cabinets to keep their belongings. The rich, in contrast, had a lot of belongings to store. They also had many rooms in which to display different objects.

The ancient Chinese sat cross-legged on woven mats and their furniture included low tables, screens, and armrests. During the Han Dynasty (206 B.C.E.–220 C.E.) in the second century C.E., the Han emperor Ling Di (156–189 C.E.) used a folding seat, known as the *huchuang*. Nomadic tribes used the seat because it could be easily folded up and carried around. The Han used the seat for hunting and traveling. Important officials and religious leaders also used low platforms to sit on during ceremonies. These seats were called *ta*. Longer platforms were also used for dining. In cold areas a hollow platform was built into the main room, known as a *kang*. Embers from the fire were placed in the hollow underneath and the family would use the *kang* for their meals and to sleep, thus keeping warm. Mats and low tables were used on the *kang*.

When Buddhism arrived in China from India, Buddhist masters sat in chairs while their disciples gathered around them sitting on stools, so the chairs were one way of marking out the masters' status. Stools, made from straw and basketwork, started to appear in ancient China beginning in the fourth century. By the time of the Tang Dynasty (618–907 C.E.),

This detail of a painting dating from the Tang Dynasty (618–907 C.E.) shows us the kind of furniture that existed in the seventh century.

A Luohanchang, or couch-bed, had three sides.

In the Ming Dynasty, a back panel higher than the side panels was considered the most elegant design.

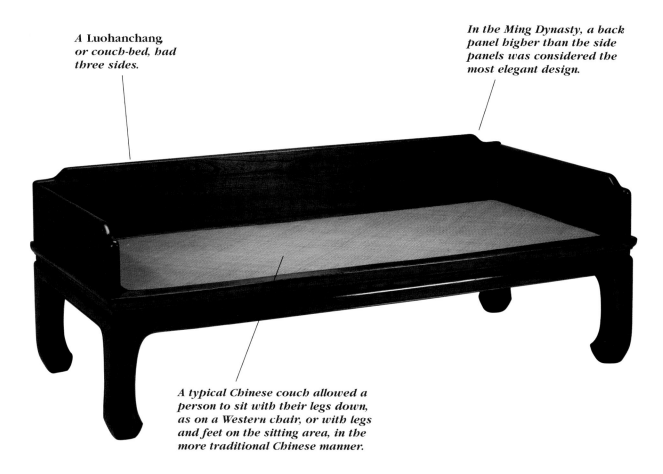

A typical Chinese couch allowed a person to sit with their legs down, as on a Western chair, or with legs and feet on the sitting area, in the more traditional Chinese manner.

This *Luohanchuang,* or couch-bed, dates from the Ming Dynasty (1368–1644 C.E.). This type of couch was used both for meeting guests and, in other areas of the house, for taking naps.

noblemen and high-ranking officials used chairs and stools. Wall paintings of the period show different kinds of chairs on which people sat either cross-legged or with their legs hanging down. There was usually a footrest to keep their feet off the cold floor. By the Song Dynasty (960–1279 C.E.) there were more different kinds of furniture available. Paintings and archaeological discoveries show that tables, chairs, stools, and benches were popular.

During the late Ming (1368–1644 C.E.) and early Qing (*Ching*) (1644–1911 C.E.) dynasties furniture became very elegant, and was made in beautiful dark hardwoods, including rosewood. Native timber, such as pine and elm, was also used. Furniture was sophisticated, and heavily influenced by the tastes of the educated classes. It was constructed with elegant curved lines and, because of their high degree of skill, the furniture-makers of the Ming Dynasty hardly ever used nails and glue.

Getting Around Ancient China

Ancient China had a system of roads, which was greatly expanded by First Emperor Qin (259–210 B.C.E.). However, in the south were there were so many rivers that it was common to travel long distances by water. Later, a sophisticated system of canals was built to provide transportation of goods between northern and southern China. The rich rode horses while porters carried women from wealthy families in covered chairs. Donkeys, mules, and, in northern China, camels were used to carry goods. Donkey and ox carts were also a common sight on the roads.

The earliest people settled along China's two major rivers, the Yellow River in northern China and the Yangtze River in southern China. In the sixth century, the two rivers were linked with the building of the Grand Canal, which covered 1,500 miles (2,415 kilometers). Emperor Yangdi (569–618 C.E.) commissioned the canal to move soldiers and grain tax around his empire. The canal was improved with the building of locks and developed over subsequent centuries. In southern China, there was a network of canals linking different cities. The urban waterways were very busy with rafts, barges, junks, and sampans floating along. Some families lived in boats on the canals. The wealthier citizens had their own boats, which were often beautifully decorated. Water taxis were also available to carry passengers.

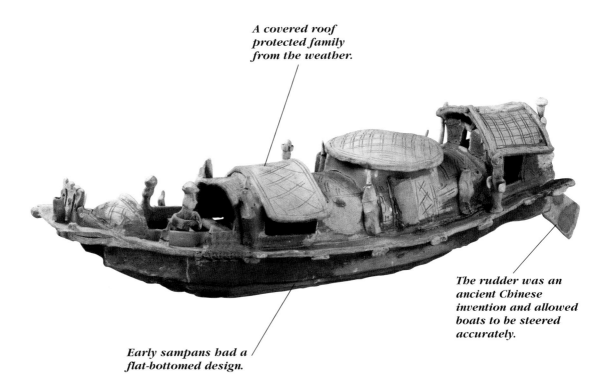

A covered roof protected family from the weather.

The rudder was an ancient Chinese invention and allowed boats to be steered accurately.

Early sampans had a flat-bottomed design.

A Han Dynasty (206 B.C.E.–220 C.E.) clay model of a typical sampan boat. Boats were an important means of transport in ancient China.

Building a Road Network

One of the many spectacular engineering achievements of First Emperor Qin was the building of a vast road network that would stretch from his capital, Xianyang *(Shee'en-yang)*, near present-day Xi'an *(Shee'ann)*, to the farthest corners of his empire. During his rule it is recorded that more than 4,000 miles (6,440 kilometers) of roads were built. The network allowed First Emperor Qin to send his soldiers to control his newly unified empire as well as transport goods more easily.

Other emperors continued to add to the road network so that by the end of the second century C.E. China had around 22,000 miles (35,400 kilometers) of roads. Where the roads crossed one of the many canals, bridges, made from wood or stone, were built to span the waterway. The Chinese also invented the first suspension bridges, made from iron chains, probably as far back as the Han Dynasty (206 B.C.E.–220 C.E.).

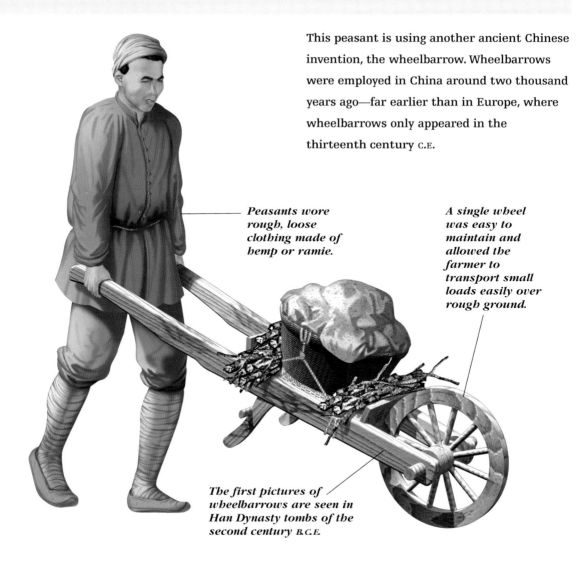

This peasant is using another ancient Chinese invention, the wheelbarrow. Wheelbarrows were employed in China around two thousand years ago—far earlier than in Europe, where wheelbarrows only appeared in the thirteenth century C.E.

Peasants wore rough, loose clothing made of hemp or ramie.

A single wheel was easy to maintain and allowed the farmer to transport small loads easily over rough ground.

The first pictures of wheelbarrows are seen in Han Dynasty tombs of the second century B.C.E.

With the building of the road network during the Qin Dynasty (221–206 B.C.E.), workers and soldiers were sent across the empire. People walked, and when they could they used the ox-drawn cart to transport agricultural goods, because horses were reserved for the wealthy or army leaders. Camels were used in the northern and the western desert, particularly along the Silk Road by merchants traveling to and from China. The earliest evidence of wheeled transportation in China dates from the Shang Dynasty (c. 1600–1050 B.C.E.). Chariots with spoked wheels were brought in from central Asia.

By the fourth century B.C.E., Chinese wheels were very advanced. Wheelwrights made the wheels with hubs and spokes to strengthen them to travel on rough terrain. Many of the wheels and chariots were made from wood, which means that they have not survived over time. In tombs of the Shang Dynasty, bronze models of horse-drawn chariots have been discovered along with the skeletons of horses buried with them. The tomb of First Emperor Qin (259–210 B.C.E.) also contains bronze chariots and clay models of chariot horses.

Money

As far back as the earliest settlements in ancient China, people used a form of money to exchange goods. The earliest currency was the shell of the cowrie, a brightly colored mollusk

The holes allowed the coins to be strung on rope or stacked on a wooden pole.

These coins have survived because they were put into a tomb for the dead person's use in the afterlife.

The first Emperor Qin standardized money during the Qin Dynasty (221–206 B.C.E.) and introduced standard round coins with a square hole, such as these.

Paper Money

The development of *jiaozi (Jee'aow-tzuh)* (paper money) resulted directly from the bonds issued to merchants for their heavy loads of coins. Starting in the seventh century, people were issuing paper bills locally, but it was not until the Song Dynasty (960–1279 C.E.) that bills started to be issued officially across China by the government in 1023 C.E. The paper bills helped ease the shortage of metals for coin making and were used along with the coins that were available.

During the Yuan Dynasty (1279–1368 C.E.), paper bills were used throughout China and were printed freely. By the fifteenth century, hyperinflation was destroying the Chinese economy because so much money was in circulation. In an effort to stop the economic meltdown and the high inflation, the Ming Dynasty (1368–1644 C.E.) stopped printing paper money. With the ending of paper money, a lot of Chinese trade with the outside world closed down.

This is an example of one of the largest paper notes in the world. It measures 13 inches by 8½ inches (338 x 220 mm) and was introduced in 1375 by Emperor Hongwu.

found in parts of Africa and Asia. By the fourth century B.C.E., bronze and copper coins were widely used. The currency came in different forms. There was spade-shaped money (based on farming tools) and knife-shaped money (based on hunting or fishing tools), as well as "ant-nose" money, which consisted of a short inscription that looked like an ant, on a small piece of bronze, which was modeled on the cowrie shells. These different kinds of money were used in regional parts of China and were often hard to come by, which gave them a high value. Miniature versions of the tools were also made and they too were highly sought after. During the Qin (221–206 B.C.E.) and Han (206 B.C.E.–220 C.E.) dynasties a coin, as we would recognize it, appeared. It was circular-shaped and became the standard form of currency. Its shape may well have come from the *bi* (*bee*), the disk of jade with a round hole in the middle, found in royal tombs. However, the production of the coin was not controlled, and so coins of different weights and sizes were circulated. The coins of the Qin Dynasty were round with a square hole in the middle so they could be threaded together. In 112 B.C.E., the Han government finally took control of the minting process and produced the *wuzhu* coin. Its name came from its inscription, which gave its weight as *wuzhu* or five grains.

Delivering the Mail

Once First Emperor Qin (259–210 B.C.E.), who reigned from 221 to 210 B.C.E., had unified the entire vast country, it was essential for him to be able send orders quickly and reliably to his commanders at the farthest reaches of his empire. During the Han Dynasty the mail system became well organized. Conscripts to the army were used as couriers to transport official mail. They worked in relays, running from one post to the next, carrying the wooden documents. However, to deliver a document as quickly as possible, horses were used. To show that the message was urgent, it was inscribed on specially shaped rods of wood to distinguish it from the usual administrative reports that were sent to and from the imperial capital. During later dynasties, messages were still conveyed on foot or horseback but were written on silk or paper.

Why Paper?

The round coin with a square hole in the middle remained the model for Chinese coins until the late nineteenth century. Other forms of currency were also used. The most common was bolts or rolls of silk, which had a monetary value. Paper bills were invented much later in response to metal shortages and for practical reasons. For example, metal coins were very heavy, which made it difficult for rich merchants to carry their money around. To avoid having to lug heavy bags of coins everywhere, merchants would leave their coins with a trustworthy person who would give the merchant a piece of paper with the amount of money written on it. When the merchant showed the slip of paper, he would be given back his money.

Chapter Four

Family Life

The basis of ancient Chinese society was the family. For the Chinese, the family was meant to include not just parents and children but the extended family that included grandparents, aunts, and uncles, and even family members who were dead. The ideal Chinese family was made up of four generations, though usually it was more likely to be three generations who lived together in the same house. As well as the living, the Chinese believed their dead ancestors continued to live with them in spirit and protected the household.

Respecting one's elders was an essential part of Chinese Confucian belief, because the Chinese held that with age came wisdom and experience. Parents were responsible for their children and this extended beyond raising them and educating them to choosing a husband or wife for them. It was the father's job, as head of the household, to tell his sons what kind of job he would do and it was the responsibility of the son to listen to his father. For girls, life in ancient China offered little opportunity beyond being a good daughter and then a dutiful wife and good mother, although some became writers and some even famous warriors.

Life in the Home
Life in ancient Chinese homes was very hierarchical, and there was a social order that had to be followed. At the head of the house was the eldest male of the oldest generation. His eldest surviving son succeeded him, and then the eldest surviving

The painter Su Hanchen (1131–1170 C.E.) painted this scene of two children playing together around 1150 C.E. We can tell they are from a wealthy family by their clothes and the furniture.

son became the next head of the household when his father died. Age was considered to be the most important thing, followed by gender. This meant the oldest male family member was the most important person but a grandmother was considered more important than her grandson because of her age and experience. Girls were the least valued members of any family.

A Chinese family included its dead ancestors as well as the living members, and every Chinese home had a shrine so the living members of the family could offer their respects to the dead members of the family on a daily basis. Each morning and evening, the family would burn incense and bow in front of either a portrait or a tablet, with the name of the ancestor written on it. They believed the smoke from the incense floated up toward the spirit of the ancestor. On special days, such as one of the many festival days, more elaborate ceremonies were held. On those days, the head of the family would pray and bow before the ancestor's portrait and each

This copy of a famous woodblock print by Lou Shou (1090–1162 C.E.) shows a rural family worshipping at their ancestor shrine.

family member, in order of seniority, would follow suit. The family would offer food to their ancestors, with the most important ancestors and those who had most recently died being offered the most. The family would then eat the food after the ceremony. Because the male family members were in charge of the family it followed that when a girl married she left her family and home and moved in with her new husband's family. They became her family and her loyalties switched to her new family.

When Is an Uncle Not an Uncle?

The Chinese language reflects the importance of family relationships. It has separate characters to distinguish "elder brother" and "younger brother," as well as "elder sister" and "younger sister." There are different words for uncle depending on whether the uncle is the "father's elder brother" or "father's younger brother," or the "mother's elder brother" or "mother's younger brother."

Families lived together in clans. In the Shang Dynasty (c. 1600–1050 B.C.E.), there were only around twenty family surnames, and families with the same name lived close to one another. This principle continued through imperial China with families of the same surname living in the same neighborhood. They would perform ceremonies together regularly to honor the first male who created their clan. Often, they would worship in the ancestral temple that the different families shared together.

Marriage

Marriage in ancient China was a family affair. The young couple was not consulted about whom they wanted to marry and often only met each other for the first time on their wedding day. For young couples from ordinary backgrounds, marriages seem to have been the end result of a large gathering of young men and women from the local neighborhood. In spring and fall, groups met. There, young men and women exchanged songs and gifts, danced together, and then married. Women were not supposed to meet men on their own, and to do so without the end result being a wedding was considered very shameful.

For the elite classes, marriage was more about bringing two families together. During the Zhou (*Joe*) Dynasty (1050–221 B.C.E.), the bride often took her sisters or cousins after she married to be secondary wives to her husband. Families did not allow chance to play a part in any prospective marriage, so they employed a *mei* (marriage arranger). It was the job of the *mei* to ensure that the two families were well matched. If a couple fell in love without the involvement of their families or the *mei*, they were often not allowed to marry because this was seen as an example of them following their own wishes and not those of their parents.

The *mei* negotiated the marriage once the prospective couple's horoscopes had been read. If the couple were well suited according to the horoscope, then a settlement had to be agreed to.

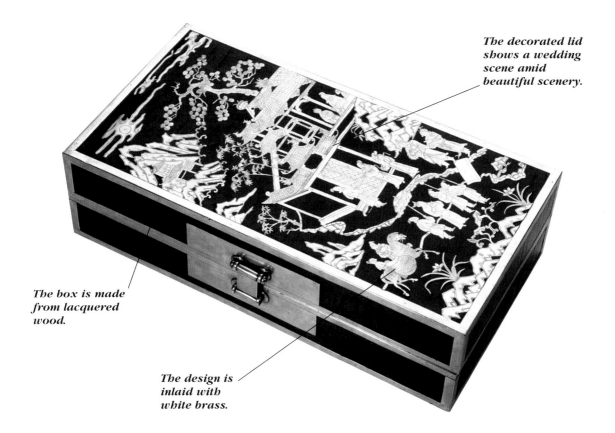

The decorated lid shows a wedding scene amid beautiful scenery.

The box is made from lacquered wood.

The design is inlaid with white brass.

Made in the Ming Dynasty between 1573 and 1619, this decorated box was used to store written agreements between two families during the wedding negotiations.

The girl's parents demanded gifts from the groom's family, which might include money, clothing, or ornaments. If they asked for too many things, the *mei* would try to find a deal that was acceptable to both parties until the two families agreed.

Brides-to-be at this time in history were given a pair of slippers made from *kudzu*, a vine that had particular uses connected with pregnancy and birth, and was seen as a sign of fertility. Wearing the slippers, the bride performed a dance that, according to legend, was first danced by Jiang Yuan, who created the Zhou people by stepping the footprints of a god and becoming pregnant. After the dance, arrows were put into a quiver, which hung from a sash around the bride's waist.

The groom then called on the bride's family. He had to wait until the evening because the Chinese character for evening, *hun*, sounds the same as the character for marriage. Also, the evening was dark and this fitted in with the Chinese concept of *yin-yang*, where the world was divided into opposites. The dark and women were both considered *yin* while the man and light were *yang*. The first duty of the groom was to make sure he and his future wife had

A colorful painted mural from the Dunhuang Caves shows us the elaborate celebrations that took place during a wedding in the Tang Dynasty (618–907 C.E.).

Su Hanchen painted many pictures of children playing at different times of the year. This image shows three children playing in a yard during the fall.

different surnames. In China, people with the same surname were not allowed to marry because they were considered to belong to the same extended family or clan. When he arrived in the evening the groom also brought a wild goose or, if possible, a pair of geese because geese are supposed to mate for life.

The wedding ceremony eventually developed into a more solemn affair. The bride was taken to the groom's house in a "bridal chair." She was supposed to "resist" as she climbed into the chair, and her face was hidden by a veil. When she arrived at the groom's house, loud music was played. The wedding ceremony itself was very simple. The bride and groom bowed to their parents and to their ancestors and were then married. The groom took his new bride back to his family home where they enjoyed a wedding banquet. After they had been married for three months, the wedding was official and the wife took on the privileges and responsibilities of her new family.

Children and Education

Having children was at the heart of ancient Chinese society. Confucius said that it was the duty of every son and daughter to have children. He wrote, "There are three ways of being unfilial and of these not begetting descendants is the most serious." The main job of a woman was to give birth and then raise her children. If, for any reason, a couple could not have children, they were expected to adopt a child or, if they could afford it, to take a concubine to have a child for them. A concubine was another wife who did not have the same rights as the first wife but who was part of the family. A man could have as many concubines as he could afford. The emperor always had the most.

Once a woman was pregnant, it was a cause for great celebration. However, the birth of sons was greeted with more joy than that of daughters. We know this because during the Shang Dynasty (c. 1600–1050 B.C.E.), the pregnancies of a woman named Fu Hao were recorded on oracle bones around 1200 B.C.E. She was a famous concubine of the king, Wu Ding, who reigned from 1250–1192 B.C.E.

On one bone it was recorded that the king predicted the birth of a daughter, which was seen as an inauspicious (unfortunate) outcome. Later, however, the birth of a daughter came to be seen as something that was not too disappointing, largely because the ancient Chinese realized that without women no sons could be born.

This Qing Dynasty (1644–1911 C.E.) painted porcelain vase shows a woman with her two children.

The process of giving birth was thought unclean, and the woman, accompanied only by her mother, had to leave the family home to give birth. When the baby was three days old, Confucian rituals were followed. In the Classic of Rites, it is stipulated that rituals should be carried out to decide which male family member should "raise up" the baby and take it from the birthing chamber. Then the mother could return home.

Educating and raising a child followed the basic belief that a baby is not born as a fully evolved human being but that every stage marks part of the process of becoming part of a family and society, as well as a good citizen. During the Han Dynasty (206 B.C.E.–220 C.E.), education became very highly regarded.

The Chinese Idea of Family

The ancient Chinese philosopher Confucius (551–479 B.C.E.) believed that the family was a miniature version of the much larger state, and that the emperor was the father of everyone. The Chinese administration followed the same strict social structure that was applied to family life. For example, the district magistrate was called in Chinese the "father and mother official." Confucius wrote much about the importance of the family and the respect the younger members must show the older members. He thought that if family members showed respect to one another, they would automatically show respect to their wider community.

Emperor Wu Di (157–87 B.C.E.) followed the belief of Confucius (551–479 B.C.E.), who said that the key to good government was through education. The emperor ordered public schools for boys to be opened across China, where the ideas of Confucius were to be taught. The Grand School opened with fifty students. One hundred years later it had more than 30,000.

Education was a crucial part of a boy's upbringing. From what we know about elite families— there are few records about life for peasant families—it was very important for a son to get a good education so he might rise through the ranks of officials. His education was made up of different parts, including calligraphy, martial arts, painting, and poetry, all of which were considered essential. A court historian named Ban Gu (32–92 C.E.), who wrote the *History of the Han Dynasty*, was supposed to have learned by heart the *Shijing* (Classic of Poetry) by the age of eight.

Girls did not have a formal education. Instead they were taught "female morals"—how to be a good daughter and wife and to respect male authority and older people—as well as singing and dancing. Some girls from noble families were taught to read and write, though this was not usual. One girl who received an education was Ban Zhou (48–116 C.E.), the sister of Ban Gu, who finished writing the *History of the Han Dynasty* started by her father and brother.

Beginning in the Tang Dynasty (618–907 C.E.) and onward, the main way of moving up in society was to pass the official government examinations. These were extremely challenging and needed a lot of study. Very few boys made the grade (the odds of becoming an official were as high as one in three thousand), but those who passed the exam entered a world of privilege.

Work

There were four main occupations in ancient China. People worked as officials, farmers, artisans, and merchants. There was a social order, which put officials at the top with the merchants at the bottom. Even though the merchants were usually the richest, they were the least respected. Above all of these were the noblemen who ruled over the others.

In ancient China the vast projects of the different emperors required a large workforce. Laborers were obliged to work for a number of days each year on civic projects. For example, most Chinese cities had high city walls around them. Peasants needed to take time off from working in the fields to construct these walls. One wall, built to surround a Shang capital, Zhengzhou (*Jung-joe*) in present-day Henan province in around fourteenth century B.C.E., was said to have taken thousands of laborers, working every day, twelve and a half years to finish.

Most ancient Chinese people worked the land. Horses were an important part of daily life and had to be cared for. This fourteenth-century painting shows grooms feeding their horses.

First Emperor Qin (259–210 B.C.E.), who reigned from 221 to 210 B.C.E., used vast numbers of workers to build border defenses and his extensive road network. He used men from the many states he conquered. His ability to mobilize great numbers of soldiers to fight his enemies was probably one of the most important factors in his conquering of all his neighbors and the emergence of a unified China in 221 B.C.E. In the same way, artisans often worked in large groups. When a bronze vessel was cast it involved a number of workers, including potters to make the mold, smelters to smelt the metals, and also, if it was very big, a lot of laborers to

Guanxi

Guanxi (Gwan-she) is a word that is untranslatable into English. It has many different meanings such as "personal contacts," "personal connections," or "reciprocal obligation." It implies a relationship where people can make unlimited demands on each other without worrying about offending the other person, and it comes from the ancient Chinese family system where members of the extended family were obliged to help each other. *Guanxi* was influenced by the Confucian idea of reciprocal obligation toward family members and was the basis of family life. It is still very important in China.

This painting from the 1100s C.E. shows a young man being called to pay respect to his elders. It is an illustration from a popular book called the *Twenty-Four Examples of Filial Piety*.

pour the liquid metal. When ceramics became popular and demand rose, large numbers of artisans were involved in the process of creating the fine china.

Good Manners

Respect for one's elders was at the heart of ancient China's social order. During the Yuan Dynasty (1279–1368 C.E.) there was a very popular book titled the *Twenty-Four Examples of Filial Piety*. It was a collection of stories that emphasized the Confucian ideal of showing respect to one's parents. In one story, Lao Laizi, who is seventy years old, keeps his parents

This large painting from the Song Dynasty (960–1279 C.E.) shows different stages from a party held in the springtime. We can see the men and their horses arriving for the party, followed by the guests enjoying different party activities including playing music and games.

happy by behaving like a child. He spends his time dancing and doing somersaults to make them laugh. In another story, a girl, Hua Mulan, joins the army to protect her old sick father and weak younger brother. She pretends to be a boy and goes in their place. For twelve years, she fights bravely without anyone discovering she is a girl.

Chapter Five

Fun and Games

For the ancient Chinese, fun and games were an important part of life, even if the majority of people had very little free time to enjoy themselves. Most Chinese had to work all day, every day, and they did not have days off. Instead, leisure was confined to national festivals, the biggest of which was the celebration that marked the Chinese New Year. The early dynasties celebrated the New Year, but not at the same time of year. It was only during the Qin Dynasty (221–206 B.C.E.) that First Emperor Qin changed the date so that the New Year was celebrated on the second new moon after the winter solstice, which is around late January or early February.

The origin of certain Chinese games, such as martial arts and flying kites, came from the battlefields. Some of the most popular ancient Chinese pastimes, such as *gongfu* (often spelled as *kung fu* in the West), which have since been taken up across the world, started thousands of years ago as people in what is now China fought against one another. Other games that originated in China include playing cards and board games, such as *weiqi* (*Wei-chee*) and *mah jong*, both of which are still played today. The Chinese invented gunpowder in the eighth century and used it for fun as well as weapons two centuries later, when firecrackers were set off to mark special days.

The First Game?

Historians think the very first game played in ancient China was an archery contest. Archaeologists discovered a bronze vessel, dating from around 1000 B.C.E., known as

This woodcut illustrates the story of the famous general Guan Yu (160–219 C.E.), who played *weiqi* **to distract himself while his physician removed a poisoned arrow from his arm.**

the *Zha Bo gui* (a *gui* is a type of vessel). The vessel, discovered in 1993, had an inscription carved on it that said that the king had a prize that he would award to the winner. Zha Bo shot at a target ten times, hitting it each time, winning the prize. In ancient China, archery was considered to be among the skills an educated man was supposed to master. The carving on the vessel suggests that archery was considered to be more than a game, although the philosopher Confucius (551–479 B.C.E.) did not agree. In fact, he risked being criticized when he said it was only a game.

Martial Arts

The earliest forms of martial arts were developed for military use, but they soon acquired a more spiritual aspect and became linked with different beliefs, especially Daoism. However, when martial arts precisely started no one can really say.

Early records such as the Classic of Rites describe a form of wrestling called *jiaodi* (*Jee'ow-dee*) (locking horns), which suggests that it was inspired by watching bulls and rams lock horns. By the time of the Han Dynasty (206 B.C.E.–220 C.E.), it was distinguished by its rules from free-for-all fighting. By this time people started to practice certain martial art movements as part of a belief in Daoism and as a means to promote health.

Martial arts developed over the following centuries. New routines were added and different theoretical texts were published. By the time of the Yuan Dynasty (1279–1368 C.E.), new martial arts skills, including fighting with different weapons, such as spears, axes, and cudgels, single- and double-edged swords, as well as broadswords, were added. Martial arts were even performed on the stage. The golden age of martial arts was during the Ming Dynasty (1368–1644 C.E.), when there were more schools of martial arts than ever before and martial arts schools flourished.

Shaolin Gongfu

Gongfu is a general name that describes all Chinese martial arts, but the most famous is that developed by the Zen Buddhist monks in Shaolin Monastery in present-day Henan province. The idea behind *Gongfu* was that to keep healthy, a person needed both inner and outer strength. Physical exercise was needed to keep the outer body strong, while breathing exercises would help to strengthen the body's inner organs and regulate their flow of *qi* (energy). By regulating and preserving *qi*, they believed, a person could gain immortality.

The monks trace their tradition back to the first patriarch of Chinese Zen Buddhism, Bodhidharma, who arrived in China from India in 528 C.E. But it is not until the sixteenth century that there are documents showing that *Gongfu* was central to the monks' life at Shaolin.

Gambling

The ancient Chinese loved games that relied on chance, and from early in their history, they invented numerous games that involved playing with cards, dice, and small tokens that could be played for money. Dice games were invented early on. As in many ancient societies, the very earliest dice were simply the knuckle bones of sheep. Later, cubic dice were made from bone, wood, or metals such as brass.

During the Han Dynasty (206 B.C.E.–220 C.E.), gambling sticks were popular. The game involved shaking wooden or bamboo sticks out of a pot onto a table. The sticks were also used to tell the future. One such game was called *liubo* (six sticks). Paintings of men playing *liubo* have been discovered on the walls of Han tombs. Unfortunately, the rules of the game disappeared by the sixth century C.E., and no record of how to play the game has ever been found. Archaeologists have discovered stone game boards, dice, and ceramic models of people playing the game, which is how historians know the game existed.

This ancient wall painting shows monks practicing gongfu, or martial arts. We can see from their posture that the exercise made them very strong and flexible.

Games and Horses

The horse was not native to China, but following its arrival, probably around 1200 B.C.E. in the latter part of the Shang Dynasty (c. 1600–1050 B.C.E.), it was adopted into Chinese military life.

By the Qin (221–206 B.C.E.) and Han (206 B.C.E.–220 C.E.) dynasties, the Chinese realized they needed divisions of mounted soldiers, or cavalry units, in order to battle the nomadic armies who fought on horseback and often threatened their borders. From the time of the Han Dynasty, men started to use horses for recreation as well as on the battlefield.

This mural from the Tang Dynasty tomb of Prince Li Xian at Qianling shows a group of nobles playing polo.

In the Tang Dynasty (618–907 C.E.) noblewomen also rode. The newly introduced game of polo, which came from Central Asia along the Silk Road, was popular with the men and women of the elite of the Tang Dynasty. Similar to field hockey on horseback, polo was a very physical sport which required great skill to play well. Many murals and clay models that have been found in the tombs of Tang imperial princes depicting the game indicate the popularity of polo. The imperial team would often challenge teams of visiting diplomats from foreign countries. Chinese women also played. There were stables at the imperial palace for the hundreds of horses used by the Tang imperial princes and princesses.

Another sport of the elite that involved horses was hunting. Mural paintings found in Tang tombs show noblemen on horseback hunting different wild animals. Hundreds of riders could participate in a hunt. As well as providing a leisure pursuit, it was good training for riders who went into battle. The murals sometimes show a hunter with a hunting dog or a large hunting cat riding on the horse with him.

How to Play Weiqi

The game of *weiqi* consists of a board divided into a grid, and one set each of black and white stones. Two players take turns to place either the black or white stones on empty intersections of the grid. The aim of the game is to take charge of a larger part of the board than your opponent. To do this, each player puts his stones on parts of the board so they cannot be captured. To capture a piece, stones of the opposite color must surround the opponent's stone. The trick is to find a balance between attacking and defending. The game is over when neither player can move any more pieces.

Board Games

The ancient Chinese invented one of the oldest board games in the world, known as *weiqi* (go). The game was extremely popular among the Chinese elite because it was very complex, despite having simple rules. There are different theories about who invented the game. One legend claims that Emperor Yao, who according to legend was supposed to have lived about 4,500 years ago, ordered one of his advisors to design a game for his son, Danzhu, who was a bit wild. The game was meant to teach him discipline, concentration, and balance. Another theory suggests *weiqi* was probably based on warfare, with each player trying to take the other's pieces.

Weiqi reached its peak of popularity during the rule of Emperor Wu, who ruled from 502 to 550 C.E. He was a huge fan of the game and played long into the night with his advisors. Emperor Wu also wrote about the game and organized a national tournament. Such was his sense of fair play that even though he took part in the tournament he did not insist on being the winner, which, as emperor, he might have done.

Chess came to China from India and was based on a game called *chanturanga*. Buddhist missionaries may have brought the game with them when they arrived in China.

This painting dating from between 600 and 800 C.E. was discovered in a tomb at Astana, near Turpan in Xinjiang province. It shows a noblewoman playing Chinese chess, or *xiangqi*.

In ancient China, it was known as *xiangqi* (*Shee'ann-chee*) or simply *qi* (*Chee*). While *weiqi* was popular with the elite, *xiangqi* was played by a large majority of the ancient Chinese. The game became popular in the Tang Dynasty (618–907 C.E.). The board was set up as two enemy countries facing each other across a river. Players moved their pieces along the lines on the board to try and capture their opponent's king. When that happened, the game was over.

Flying Kites

It is believed that the Chinese invented kites about three thousand years ago. In 478 B.C.E., the Chinese philosopher Mozi (c. 480–397 B.C.E.) spent three years working on a wooden bird, which he flew. Why the Chinese invented the kite remains unclear, though there are many theories about how kites came to be made. They did produce the ideal materials—bamboo and silk—for making kites. Both are light enough to catch the wind and to fly. The different theories about how kites were invented include one story about a man's hat being blown from his head and then caught on the wind so it flew. Other theories suggest the idea for a kite came from watching the sails of ships, and another that banners were strengthened with bamboo so they flew more readily.

During the Han Dynasty (206 B.C.E.–220 C.E.) kites were used on the battlefield to frighten the enemy. In 200 B.C.E., Chinese general Han Xin, who died in 196 B.C.E., flew a kite over a castle to which his troops were laying siege. By measuring the length of the kite line that flew over the castle he was able to

This cylindrical bamboo container holds gambling sticks. As well as being used for gambling, the sticks were also used to tell fortunes. Future events were predicted by "reading" the first stick to be shaken out of the bamboo holder.

work out how far his men would need to tunnel under the fortress to gain access to it. Another general, in an effort to scare his enemy, fitted kites with harps and flew them over the enemy's camp. When they started to make a wailing sound, a rumor went around the camp that the gods were warning them they would lose the battle the following day. The people were so scared they fled. Another use for kites during wartime was to send signals to troops on the battlefield. It is said that the ancient Chinese even built large kites that could carry warriors, armed with bows and arrows, to shoot at the enemy.

The use of kites changed with the invention of paper in the Han Dynasty. Until then kites had only been made from silk. However, once the process of making paper became less expensive, it meant that paper kites could be made cheaply. During the Tang Dynasty, kites were flown for pleasure by the wealthy. They became more affordable for ordinary people during the Song Dynasty (960–1279 C.E.).

Kite flying was a popular pastime for children as well as adults. As the ancient Chinese learned more about making kites they became more sophisticated. In this embroidered silk design, we can see children flying many different shaped kites.

The earliest shape of the kite was a flat rectangle. Over time, this became much more complicated as kites became three-dimensional. Kites were made in many different shapes, which had a symbolic meaning. For example, tortoises, cranes, and peaches represented

A Health Benefit

The ancient Chinese believed that flying kites would bring good fortune and avoid bad luck, and that the higher the kite flew, the more money they would get. They also believed that by looking up at the flying kite, they improved their eyesight, and by tilting the head backward to watch the kite and opening the mouth slightly, they got rid of extra heat from their mouth and balanced their body's *yin-yang*.

A great crowd of spectators watches four different sports at a Chinese frontier camp. In the center, men can be seen wrestling, a pastime which led to the development of Chinese martial arts.

long life, while butterflies and flowers meant harmony, bats meant good luck, and the dragon, one of the most popular, represented wealth and power. Kites were flown on many occasions to celebrate one of a number of Chinese holidays, for religious reasons, and for special family occasions.

One popular festival, dating from the Song Dynasty, was the *Chongyang* (Double Nine) Festival. Its name came from the festival held each year on the ninth day or the ninth lunar month. Each family would fly a kite to remember their ancestors. Once the kite was high in the sky, the family cut the kite line and allowed it to fly away. It was believed that the kite took away sickness and bad luck from the family. It was considered very bad luck, however, if the kite fell back down to earth and landed on a house.

Fireworks

Gunpowder, used to make fireworks, was invented in China. According to a popular Chinese legend, fireworks were discovered by accident when a cook mixed together charcoal, sulfur, and saltpeter, which were all used in the kitchens of ancient China. The mixture was heated over a fire and then dried to make a black flaky powder. When the powder was set on fire it exploded with a loud bang.

The ancient Chinese called this *huo yao* (fire chemical). They experimented with this early gunpowder by putting it into the hollow of a bamboo stick and throwing it on a fire. The mixture exploded and blew apart the stick. That was how the first firecracker was made, but no one has been able to agree on the precise date when this happened. Some historians date it to about two thousand years ago, while other historians think it did not happen until the Song Dynasty (960–1279 C.E.). The confusion may have been caused by the difference in dates between the discovery of gunpowder and the invention of the firecracker.

Acrobats and Jugglers

The ancient Chinese enjoyed many kinds of entertainment, including acrobatic displays and juggling. Acrobats had been practicing their art for a long time, probably as early as the third century B.C.E., by which time they had already acquired highly advanced skills, such as jumping, tumbling, balancing, and juggling, as well as walking on ropes stretched above the ground.

During the Six Dynasties Period (220–589 C.E.), there is evidence of acrobats who could juggle seven daggers while walking on 10-foot (3-meter) stilts. We know about acrobats and their skills because brick paintings and stone engravings, dating back to the Han Dynasty (206 B.C.E.–220 C.E.), show all kinds of acrobats performing tricks.

Celebrating with Gunpowder

Throughout many dynasties the firecracker has been a key part of many Chinese celebrations. The ancient Chinese believed that the firecracker's loud bangs could scare away evil spirits. They used firecrackers to celebrate births, weddings, birthdays, and to commemorate deaths. The Chinese New Year was celebrated by setting off lots of firecrackers so that no evil spirits would travel into the New Year.

This painting shows a family setting off firecrackers to honor the stove god. Beginning in the Tang Dynasty (618–907 C.E.), many ancient Chinese believed that the stove god made a report to heaven each year about how well the family had behaved.

This terracotta vase dates back to the Han Dynasty (206 B.C.E.–220 C.E.). Although it is quite simple and unglazed, it is unusual because of the acrobats that balance on its rim.

Performances were not just for the emperor and the rich, but were often held for members of the public in street festivals. *Paixi* (*Pie-shee*) (folk festivals), which included acrobatic displays, also had musical performances, juggling, and fire eating.

During the Tang Dynasty (618–907 C.E.), acrobats were popular court entertainers. Lavish banquets, held in vast, ornately decorated halls with hundreds of guests, were common. The guests were entertained by large troupes of dancers, acrobats, and jugglers while musicians performed. Many of the acrobatic troupes came from abroad along the Silk Road and some even performed on the backs of camels. Acrobats were known to be part of the birthday celebrations for Emperor Xuanzong (*Shoo'ann-tzong*) (685–762 C.E.), who reigned from 712 to 756 C.E. Acrobatic acts performed at dinners included swallowing knives, breathing or spitting fire, and walking tightropes. Many of these acts were taken to Japan during the Tang Dynasty, where they became very popular.

Puppets

Puppet shows were another popular form of entertainment for both rich and poor. Historians believe that puppet shows date back three thousand years. One form of puppet show was the shadow puppet show, where a wooden puppet was held up against a bright light to produce a shadow. The audience watched the shadow on the background, giving the show its name.

Puppetry probably started during the Han Dynasty (206 B.C.E.–220 C.E.) but became popular during the Song Dynasty (960–1279 C.E.). There were all kinds of puppets: shadow puppets on sticks, powder puppets, and "flesh" puppets. Powder puppets came out of small pouches that were opened by a flash of gunpowder. "Flesh puppets" were actually children, who were dressed up and carried on the shoulders of adults.

As with kites and firecrackers, puppets had a symbolic function and were often used at funerals and other ceremonies. The head of a puppet was usually made from wood, and the body from wood or wire, while the limbs had joints made from leather. The feet and hands were wooden and had moveable parts. The puppet was held by at least five threads attached to a crosspiece, though there could be as many as twenty-eight threads. Part of the puppet master's skill was in preventing all the threads from getting twisted during a performance.

Everyday Life in Ancient China

At first glance, it might appear as if modern China has little in common with ancient China. What is remarkable, however, is that many of the foundations of daily life remain little changed. The way the modern Chinese live today dates back more than two thousand years to the time of Confucius. He laid down basic principles about family life, which emphasized respect for one's elders and serving the family above oneself. The position of women in ancient China was extremely restricted. Today, although the modern city women seem to enjoy more freedoms than their grandmothers, they are still limited by Chinese society's expectations of them.

China continues to be a predominantly agricultural country. The majority of people live in the countryside and grow their crops just as their ancestors did centuries ago. Despite the fast pace of change in the cities, rural China is much like it was hundreds of years ago.

Glossary of Names

Ban Gu court historian and poet who continued the work of his father, Ban Biao, in writing a history of the Han Dynasty

Ban Zhou sister of Ban Gu and the first female Chinese historian, who completed her brother's history of the Han Dynasty after he died

Cao Cao Han Dynasty military official and King of the Wei

Confucius Chinese thinker and philosopher whose teachings and beliefs about compassion, loyalty, respect, sincerity, justice, and the ideal behavior of individuals, family, government, and society as a whole form the basis of Confucianism

Danzhu son of the legendary Emperor Yao; according to one story, Yao invented the ancient game of *weiqi* (also known as *go*) to keep his son Danzhu amused and out of mischief

Emperor Yao legendary ruler who is said to have invented the game of *weiqi* (also known as *go*)

Fu Hao one of many concubines to Wu Ding, ruler of the Shang Dynasty

Han Xin military commander who served under Liu Bang (Emperor Gaozu), the first emperor of the Han Dynasty

Hua Mulan fictional young woman in Chinese legend who disguises herself as a man to take her elderly father's place in the army

Hongwu founder and first ruler of the Ming Dynasty

Huang Di (Yellow Emperor) legendary Chinese emperor and father of traditional Chinese medicine

Huizong eighth ruler of the Song Dynasty; a poet, painter, calligrapher, and musician, he wrote the *Daguanchalun* (Treatise on Tea).

Jia Sixie farming expert during the Northern Wei Dynasty; he wrote China's first agricultural encyclopedia, *Essential Skills for the Common People*

Jiang Yuan legendary woman in Chinese mythology who, after years of being childless, walked in the footprints of a god and became pregnant

Lao Laizi character whose respect for his elders is described in *Twenty-Four Examples of Filial Piety*, stories chosen and compiled by Guo Jujing during the Yuan Dynasty

Ling Di ruler of the Han Dynasty from 156 to 189 C.E.

Lu Yu Buddhist priest during the Tang Dynasty and author of *The Classic Art of Tea*

Mozi philosopher during the Warring States Period whose system of beliefs based on ideas of universal love and care for all humans became known as moism

Shen Nong legendary figure in Chinese mythology, known as the "Divine Farmer," believed to have given the gifts of agricultural knowledge and herbal medicine

Shi Huangdi founder and first ruler of the Qin Dynasty, which unified China for the first time

Wen Zhengming leading painter, calligrapher, and scholar during the Ming Dynasty

Wu Di seventh emperor of the Han Dynasty who greatly increased China's territory and organized a strong, centralized Confucian state

Wu Ding ruler of the Shang Dynasty from 1250 to 1192 B.C.E.

Xuanzong seventh and longest-reigning emperor of the Tang Dynasty

Xunzi Confucian philosopher who lived during the Warring States Period

Yangdi second ruler of the Sui Dynasty who was responsible for a large building program, including the Great Canal, rebuilding the Great Wall, and constructing roads, palaces, and ships

Zhengzong third emperor of the Song Dynasty and the third son of Emperor Taizong (Li Shimin)

Glossary

Alum aluminium potassium sulfate, a chemical used in cosmetics and with many other uses

Calligraphy the art of fine, stylized, or artistic handwriting using a pen or a brush and ink; considered as important as painting in Chinese culture

Caravanserai inn or oasis along a trade route where caravans (groups of travelers journeying together, and all their luggage and equipment) rest overnight

Concubine additional wife living with a man of higher social status, but who does not have the status and legal rights of an official wife

Dynasty succession or series of rulers who descend from the same family

Elite section of society or group of people considered superior in social, economic, or intellectual status

Etiquette standards of good behavior or expected procedure to be followed on social or official occasions

Filial piety person's love, respect, and duty toward his or her parents, grandparents, and ancestors

Hemp tall cultivated plant with tough fibers that are used to make rope, paper, canvas, and other textiles

Hierarchical arranged in increasing levels or positions of relative importance or power according to social position, wealth, or professional status

Horoscope chart or diagram showing the position of the sun, moon, and planets relative to the signs of the zodiac at a specific time, used by astrologers to provide information about a person's character and personality, and to predict his or her future

Hyperinflation continual very high rise in the general price for goods and services over a very time, so that ever greater sums of money are needed to buy the same amount

Junk type of Chinese ship with several masts, a high stern (rear), a projecting bow (front), and a large rudder for steering

Kohl cosmetic made from soot used as an eyeliner or to darken eyebrows

Lacquered coated with a smooth clear glossy varnish

Loess layer of yellow, brown, pink, or gray sediment or soil made up mostly of silt and clay, with a little sand, deposited over time by the action of the wind

Millet type of cereal grass grown for its grain, which is used for food

Nomadic person who travels and moves from place to place, often as part of a group, without a permanent home, usually following a seasonal pattern and within a certain region

Plaque decorative badge worn as an ornament or to show membership of a group

Ramie type of Asian nettle with strong, woody fibers used to make thread, fishing nets, matting, and fabrics

Saltpeter potassium nitrate or sodium nitrate, used in gunpowder and explosives

Sampan type of small flat-bottomed boat

Siege surrounding of a town, city, fortress, or castle by an enemy force, to prevent any supplies or troops going in, in order to capture or destroy it

Steppe flat and mostly treeless area of grassland, found in parts of Central Asia, southeastern Europe, and Siberia

Sulfur pale yellow nonmetallic element widely found in nature; an ingredient of gunpowder and with many other uses

Thatched covered with thatch, a type of roof covering made of straw, reeds, bulrushes, or similar

Wok deep rounded iron cooking utensil, shaped like a wide bowl

Yang male aspect of the universal energy or life force (*qi*) represented by light, heat, and dryness

Yin feminine aspect of the universal energy or life force (*qi*) represented by darkness, coolness, and wetness

Learn More About

Books

Allan, Tony. *Ancient China (Cultural Atlas for Young People)*. New York: Chelsea House Publications, 2007

Art, Suzanne Strauss. *The Story of Ancient China*. Lincoln, Mass: Pemblewick Press, 2001

Art, Suzanne Strauss. *China's Later Dynasties*. Lincoln, Mass: Pemblewick Press, 2002

Benn, Charles. *China's Golden Age: Everyday Life in the Tang Dynasty*. New York: Oxford University Press, 2004

Birch, Cyril. *Tales from China (Oxford Myths and Legends)*. New York: Oxford University Press, 2000

Challen, Paul. *Life in Ancient China (Peoples of the Ancient World)*. New York: Crabtree PC, 2004

Cotterell, Arthur & Buller, Laura. *Ancient China (DK Eyewitness Books)*. New York: Dorling Kindersley, 2005

Hollihan-Elliot, Sheila. *Ancient History Of China (History and Culture of China)*. Broomall, PA: Mason Crest Publishers, 2005

Mann, Elizabeth. *The Great Wall: The Story of Thousands of Miles of Earth and Stone that Turned a Nation into a Fortress (Wonders of the World)*. New York: Mikaya, 2006

Murowchick, Robert E. C*hina: Ancient Culture, Modern Land (Cradles of Civilization)*. Norman, Okla: University of Oklahoma Press, 1994

Schomp, Virginia. *The Ancient Chinese (People of the Ancient World)*. New York: Franklin Watts, 2005

Temple, Robert. *The Genius of China: 3,000 Years of Science, Discovery, and Invention*. Rochester, VT: Inner Traditions, 2007

Web Sites

British Museum—Ancient China
www.ancientchina.co.uk

British Museum—Early Imperial China
www.earlyimperialchina.co.uk

China Knowledge—Chinese History
www.chinaknowledge.de/History/history.htm

Gol27—History of Tea
www.gol27.com/HistoryTeaChina.html

Mr Donn—Everyday Life in Tang Dynasty China
http://china.mrdonn.org/tang.html

National Palace Museum, Taiwan
www.npm.gov.tw/en/collection/selections_01.htm

Oracle - Thinkquest—History of Chinese Clothing
http://library.thinkquest.org/05aug/01780/clothing/history.htm

University of Pittsburgh—Chinese Folk Tales
www.pitt.edu/~dash/china.html

University of Washington—Chinese Civilisation and Culture
http://depts.washington.edu/chinaciv/contents.htm

Index